ON THE HUNT

Duck HUNTING

BY ROXANNE TROUP

EPIC

BELLWETHER MEDIA • MINNEAPOLIS, MN

EPIC

EPIC BOOKS are no ordinary books. They burst with intense action, high-speed heroics, and shadows of the unknown. Are you ready for an Epic adventure?

This edition first published in 2025 by Bellwether Media, Inc.

No part of this publication may be reproduced in whole or in part without written permission of the publisher. For information regarding permission, write to Bellwether Media, Inc., Attention: Permissions Department, 6012 Blue Circle Drive, Minnetonka, MN 55343.

Library of Congress Cataloging-in-Publication Data

LC record for Duck Hunting available at: https://lccn.loc.gov/2024037674

Text copyright © 2025 by Bellwether Media, Inc. EPIC and associated logos are trademarks and/or registered trademarks of Bellwether Media, Inc.

Editor: Elizabeth Neuenfeldt   Designer: Jeffrey Kollock

Printed in the United States of America, North Mankato, MN.

TABLE OF CONTENTS

TESTING THE DECOYS	4
WHAT IS DUCK HUNTING?	6
BEFORE THE HUNT	12
SUPPORTING HABITATS	18
GLOSSARY	22
TO LEARN MORE	23
INDEX	24

TESTING THE DECOYS

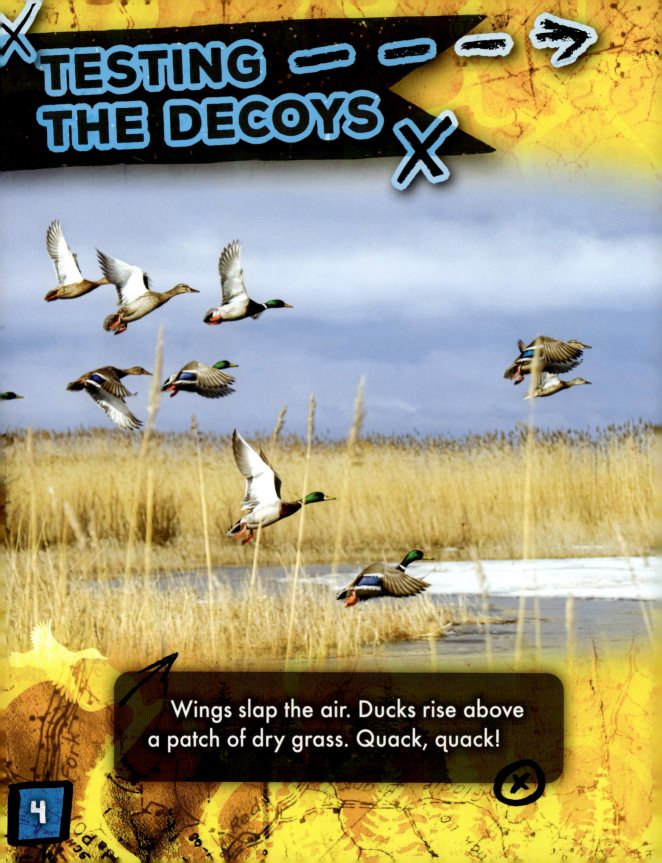

Wings slap the air. Ducks rise above a patch of dry grass. Quack, quack!

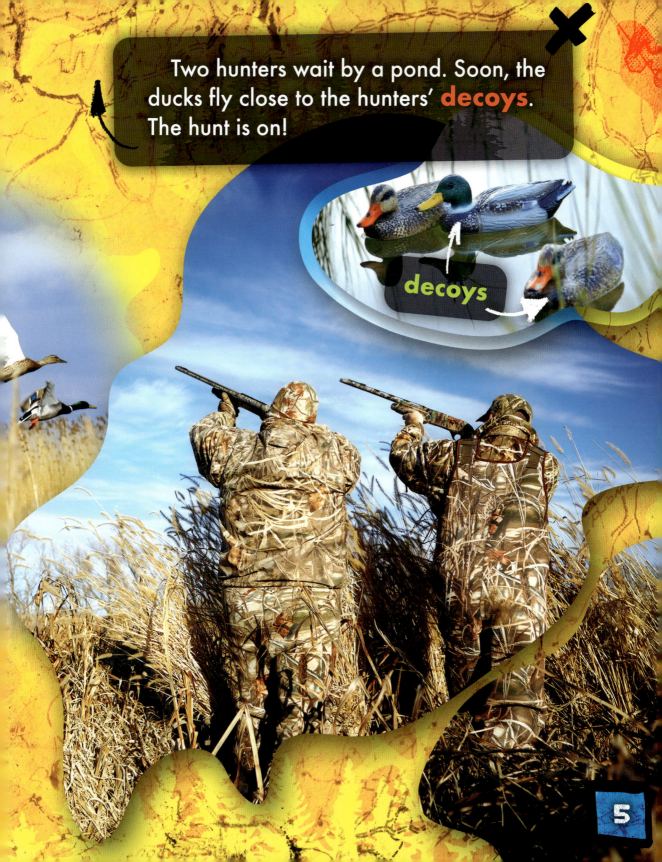

Two hunters wait by a pond. Soon, the ducks fly close to the hunters' **decoys**. The hunt is on!

decoys

WHAT IS DUCK HUNTING?

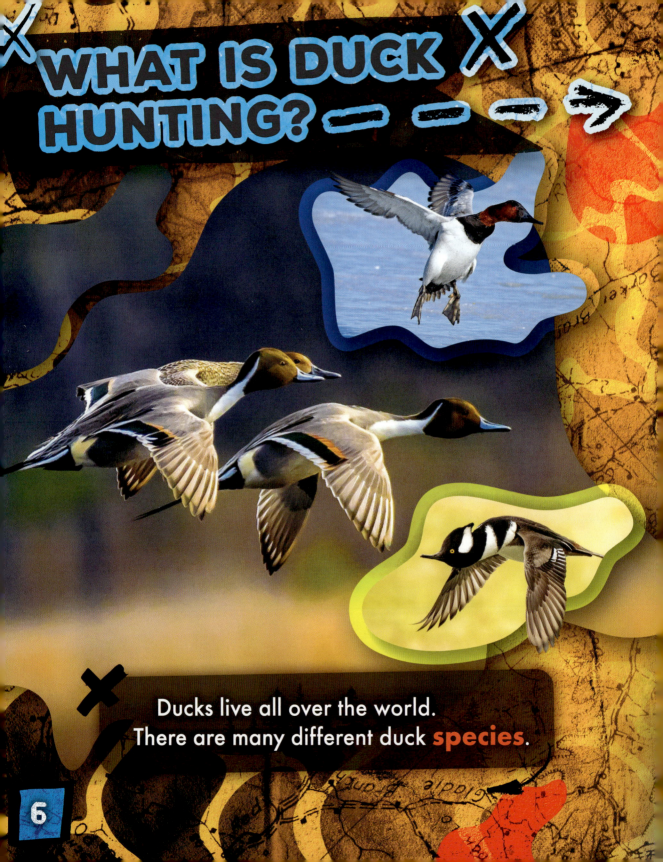

Ducks live all over the world. There are many different duck **species**.

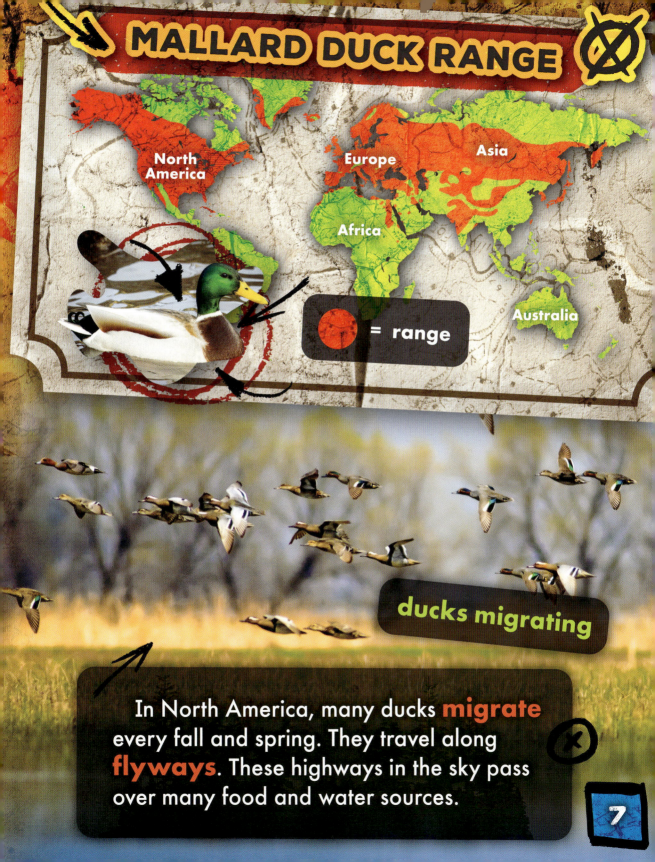

MALLARD DUCK RANGE

North America · Europe · Asia · Africa · Australia

● = range

ducks migrating

In North America, many ducks **migrate** every fall and spring. They travel along **flyways**. These highways in the sky pass over many food and water sources.

People hunt ducks in the fall and winter. They often hunt along flyways.

blind

Some people hunt in fields. Others hunt near bodies of water. They hide in brush or set up **blinds**.

People hunt ducks for different reasons. Many hunters like being outside with friends. They enjoy working with a **bird dog**. Others hunt ducks to eat them.

FAVORITE HUNTING SPOT

Arkansas

STUTTGART, ARKANSAS

✓ Known as "The Duck Capital of the World"

✓ Located along the Mississippi Flyway

BEFORE - - - - →
THE HUNT

camouflage

Duck hunters wear **camouflage** to stay hidden. They wear hats and gloves to stay warm.

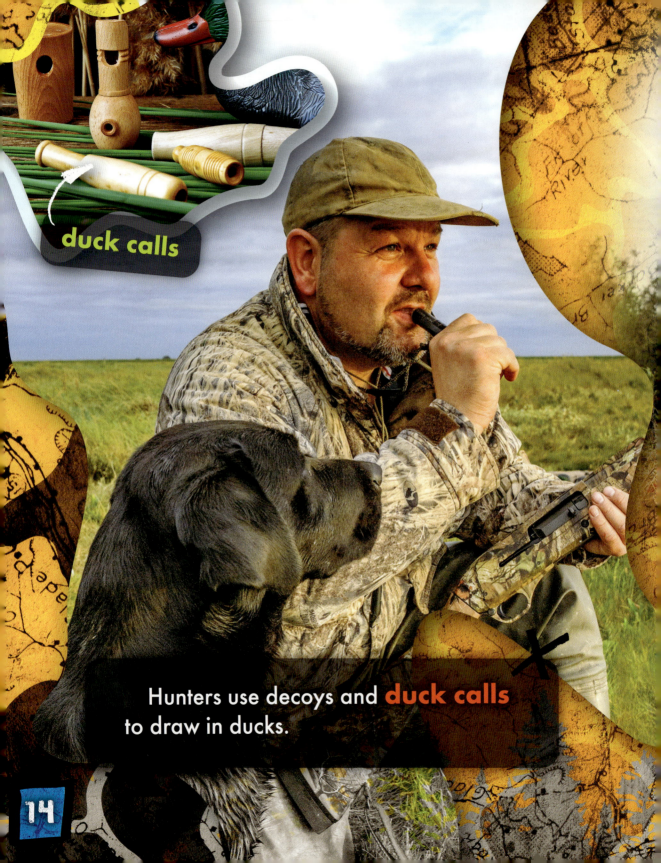

duck calls

Hunters use decoys and **duck calls** to draw in ducks.

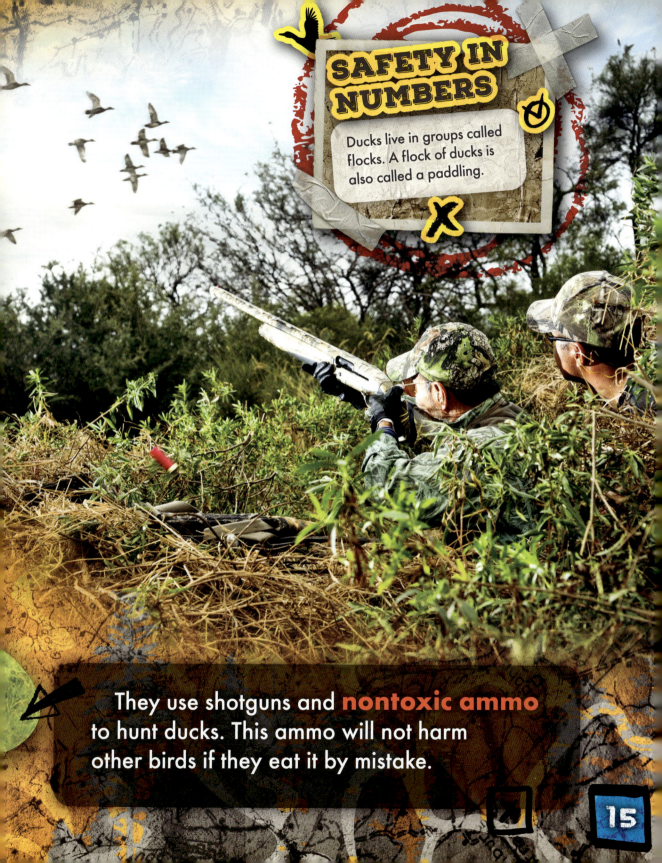

SAFETY IN NUMBERS

Ducks live in groups called flocks. A flock of ducks is also called a paddling.

They use shotguns and **nontoxic ammo** to hunt ducks. This ammo will not harm other birds if they eat it by mistake.

fetching

Many hunters bring a bird dog to help them hunt. Bird dogs are trained to **fetch** ducks without damaging the meat.

Labrador retrievers are popular bird dogs. German shorthaired pointers are popular, too.

SUPPORTING HABITATS

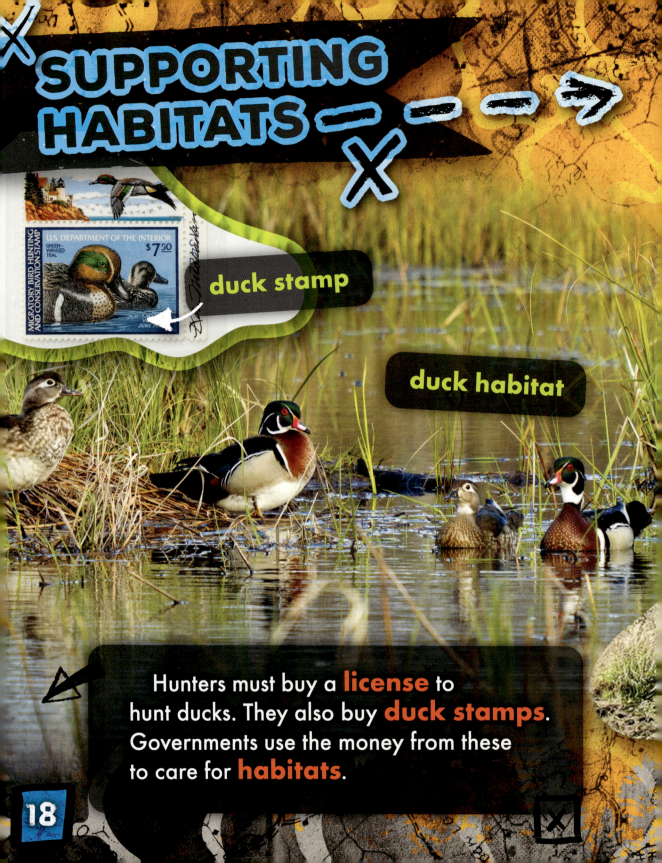

duck stamp

duck habitat

Hunters must buy a **license** to hunt ducks. They also buy **duck stamps**. Governments use the money from these to care for **habitats**.

DUCK STAMP SUCCESS!

People began buying duck stamps in 1934. Since then, around $800 million has been raised to help habitats!

Governments also limit the number and kind of ducks that can be hunted.

Most states require hunters to take a safety class before hunting. The class teaches gun safety and hunting laws. People learn to take **ethical shots**.

Hunters should not bring untrained dogs in the field. Keeping everyone safe makes duck hunting fun!

hunting safety class

HIGH-SPEED FLYER

On average, ducks can fly 40 to 60 miles (64 to 97 kilometers) per hour. But they can fly much faster for short distances!

GLOSSARY

bird dog—a dog trained to help hunters find and retrieve birds

blinds—small huts or closed spaces in which hunters wait

camouflage—a fabric that uses colors and patterns to blend in with surroundings

decoys—models of ducks used to attract real ducks

duck calls—noisemakers that copy the sounds ducks make

duck stamps—stamps required on duck hunting licenses for hunters over 16 years of age

ethical shots—clean shots that reduce pain and suffering to animals

fetch—to bring back

flyways—the paths birds fly as they migrate

habitats—the places where animals live

license—a document that gives hunters legal permission to harvest a certain type of animal

migrate—to travel from one place to another, often with the seasons

nontoxic ammo—ammo made with material that is not poisonous to animals

species—kinds of animals

TO LEARN MORE

AT THE LIBRARY

Nelson, Sarah. *Follow the Flyway: The Marvel of Bird Migration*. Concord, Mass.: Barefoot Books, 2023.

Roe, Monica. *Duck Hunting Dreams*. North Mankato, Minn.: Capstone, 2021.

Troup, Roxanne. *Pheasant Hunting*. Minneapolis, Minn.: Bellwether Media, 2025.

ON THE WEB

Factsurfer.com gives you a safe, fun way to find more information.

1. Go to www.factsurfer.com.

2. Enter "duck hunting" into the search box and click 🔍.

3. Select your book cover to see a list of related content.

INDEX

bird dog, 10, 11, 16, 17, 20

blinds, 9

camouflage, 12

decoys, 5, 14

duck calls, 14

duck stamps, 18, 19

ethical shots, 20

fall, 7, 8

favorite hunting spot, 10

fields, 9, 20

flocks, 15

fly, 5, 21

flyways, 7, 8

food, 7

gloves, 12

governments, 18, 19

habitats, 18, 19

hats, 12

hunters, 5, 10, 12, 13, 14, 16, 18, 20

hunting gear, 13

laws, 20

license, 18

migrate, 7

nontoxic ammo, 15

North America, 7

pond, 5

range, 6, 7

safety, 20

shotguns, 15

species, 6

spring, 7

states, 20

waders, 13

water, 7, 9

winter, 8

The images in this book are reproduced through the courtesy of: Mircea Costina, cover; fotoslaz, p. 3; Beegu, p. 4; CLP Media, p. 5; Aqeela_Image, p. 5 (decoys); Ryan Narron, p. 6; Brian E Kushner, p. 6 (top inset); VINEETH RADHAKRISHNAN, p. 6 (bottom inset); smutan, p. 7; Mariia Zarai, p. 7 (mallard); Brian N Rogers, p. 8; Maria Dryfhout, p. 9; Jason Lindsey/ Alamy, p. 11; Steve Oehlenschlager, pp. 11 (inset), 12; gnatoutdoors, p. 13; BearFotos, p. 13 (shotgun); Cody Stearman, p. 13 (camouflage); Cavan-Images, p. 13 (decoys); dasytnik, p. 13 (duck call); Matt Limb OBE/ Alamy, p. 14; Vasileios Karafillidis, p. 14 (duck calls); Steve Ikeguchi, p. 15; Juniors Bildarchiv GmbH/ Alamy, p. 16; Michael Parker Outdoors, p. 17; Linda Freshwaters Arndt/ Alamy, p. 18; B Christopher/ Alamy, p. 18 (duck stamp); izzet cakalli, p. 19; US Air Force/ USAF, p. 20; RubberBall/ Alamy, p. 21; Volodymyr Krasyuk, p. 23.